THE GHOSTLY TALES OF THE TREASURE COAST

Published by Arcadia Children's Books
A Division of Arcadia Publishing
Charleston, SC
www.arcadiapublishing.com

First published 2022

Manufactured in the United States

ISBN 978-1-4671-9876-9

Library of Congress Control Number: 2022934565

All images used courtesy of Shutterstock.com.

Spooky America

The Ghostly Tales of The Treasure Coast

SELENA FRAGASSI

Adapted from *Ghosts of the Treasure Coast* by Patrick S. Mesmer and Patricia A. Mesmer

arcadia CHILDREN'S BOOKS

Georgia
Jacksonville
Atlantic Ocean
Florida
Gulf of Mexico
Orlando
Tampa
Miami
1
2
3
4
5
6
7
8
9
10
11
13

Table of Contents & Map Key

Introduction

Bold pirates, brutal shipwrecks, and a bounty of gold buried deep under the sea. Welcome to Florida's Treasure Coast, located on the edge of the vast Atlantic Ocean! This part of the state is known for its lush beaches, eternal sunshine, and sunny weather. But with paradise comes plenty of folklore and many haunted experiences lurking in the shadows.

This part of Florida, discovered by explorer Juan Ponce de Léon in the year 1513, was a major—and dangerous—shipping route centuries ago. Ships carried goods and jewels

from the Caribbean to Spain. There were swashbuckling pirate takeovers and severe storms (it's called Hurricane Alley for a reason!) that left ships and valuables way down on the ocean floor.

More and more, those treasures are being discovered, as are the many haunted stories that have been buried for just as long.

For the Treasure Coast, it all begins with an ancient people called the Ais whose unusual rituals and connection to the otherworld may have set the stage for ongoing supernatural activity in this part of the country.

CHAPTER 1

The Ancient Ais People

Long before Christopher Columbus found his way to the Americas in 1492, and even before Spanish explorer Juan Ponce de Léon discovered the Treasure Coast in 1513, this area of Florida was occupied by two native peoples—the Ais and the Jeaga. It's said they had been living here since 800 BCE—nearly 3,000 years ago! Of course, there's no eyewitnesses to hand down stories about these ancient people, but they did leave plenty of remnants of their lives behind that help us piece together their stories. They were so important to the history of the Treasure Coast that old maps refer to the area as "Land of the Ais." The body of water that weaves through the land—today known as the Indian River—was once called Rio de Ais.

The Ais people lived fully and simply off the land—they fished and hunted for their food, which was plentiful. And they grew accustomed to the quickly changing weather conditions in Florida, from dealing with annoying mosquitos to creating shelter that would keep them safe during powerful storms.

The Ais people were clever—after they ate animals and shellfish, they put the leftover bones and shells in a pile and covered it with sand and dirt. They did this again and again until they formed large mounds called *middens*. (In a separate area, they also piled the bodies of their fellow tribespeople who had died, forming burial mounds.)

The middens became very large and towered high above the ground, so much so that the Ais would build shelters on top, to protect them from flooding. It also gave them a spot to perform religious rituals and ceremonies. They believed that being high off the ground would get them closer to the gods they worshiped, as well as connect them to their departed loved ones and ancestors. Even thousands of years later, many of these middens are left and they are ripe with hauntings—the Ais had some elaborate and extreme ceremonies (someone today might even call it witchcraft).

The Ais believed that people had three souls within them: in the pupil of their eyes, the shadows they cast on the ground, and in the reflections they made when standing over water. The Ais believed that the soul in the all-seeing eye would exist even after death. They would look the deceased in the eye to gain knowledge. The other two souls they believed were transferred to animals—and even when those animals eventually died, the souls would transfer again to a smaller animal. If someone in the tribe became sick, the people thought this meant one of their souls escaped and they'd consult a tribe doctor to help restore it.

When someone died, the ceremonies that followed were a very important part of Ais life. They believed that spirits were always around them, and the Ais wanted to make sure their loved ones safely made their journey to the afterlife.

One story passed down is that, once a burial mound was large enough, one of the elder tribesmen would stand on top of it and shoot an arrow into the sky. Where that arrow landed determined where to build the next mound.

They'd then take the body of someone who had just died and lay it in the new spot, covering it with some sand taken from the original mound.

Women from the tribe would visit the burial mound daily for many months and mourn the lost souls. As you can imagine, this was a very emotional experience. A lot of that energy still remains in these places. It's said that if you get close to where a mound once was, you can feel an eeriness like the Ais are watching over the sacred land. Sometimes they say you can hear the faint sound of crying still.

Another legend is that there was an Ais girl who was so sad over her brother's death during battle that he came back one day—seen as a big black mass that rose up from the ocean. He grabbed her and they disappeared back into the water. It's said that every one-hundred years this dark spirit comes back to claim another unhappy person and bring them to the happier afterlife.

The Ais people lived like this in great numbers on the Treasure Coast until about 1750 when European settlers arrived and brought with them diseases like smallpox. With no immunity to these new diseases, many, many tribespeople died. There were also many battles between the native peoples and Europeans. Those Ais who were not killed in battle were often enslaved by the Europeans.

So many of them did not have a peaceful ending to

this life. That great sorrow and suffering can be felt as you walk through the Treasure Coast, where you are literally stepping over the burial sites of these deeply spiritual people.

It's said the Ais still roam and keep a watchful eye on their land, which has led many to believe the area is haunted.

CHAPTER 2

The Disaster of 1715

The many surfers, beach lovers, and sailboat adventurers who love to take to the blue waters of the Treasure Coast may not fully realize what lurks beneath or what once rocked upon the waves centuries ago. Although it looks like paradise today, these waters have seen countless tragedies over the years. Sometimes, under the bright moonlight, people swear they see one of the souls who lost their lives to the sea many moons ago. They are still wandering the sandy beaches—but what are they looking for?

Back in the 18th century, the Treasure Coast was traveled by Treasure Fleets, or large ships that brought valuable goods from the Americas and Asia back to their homeland of Spain.

The vessels would be loaded up with goods and resources like gold, silver, sugar, tobacco, and spices, and leave from a busy shipping port in nearby Havana, Cuba to head home to Europe.

Around this time, in 1715, a long war in Europe had just ended and Spain had lost a lot of money. King Philip V of Spain had recently married. His new wife demanded that her family be given a "dowry" or lavish gifts in exchange for her hand in marriage. The only problem was that the bright emeralds and pearls she wanted were stuck on the Treasure Fleets near the Americas. The ships had been unable to return to Spain due to the long war. But with his new wife demanding her family's gifts, King Philip ordered the ships to come home.

Rushing the trip was a bad idea. After sailing for a few days under clear skies, the weather soon turned. Hurricane-force winds blew in and rocked the ships. The captains couldn't control the large vessels and they crashed near the shoreline of what's now called the Sebastian Inlet on the Treasure Coast. They crashed with such force that it was like the ships exploded, breaking into

thousands of pieces and sending passengers overboard. Some swam and made it to shore—even with grave injuries. Others died from drowning or were eaten by sharks. And yet others had been crushed by broken parts of the ship. The site looked like a war zone. There were about 1,500 stranded people stretching across miles of beach who were hurt and confused. With no shade or shelter, they were burned by the sun and bitten by insects. With no food or fresh water, many died after a few days. Those who survived were clinging to life when rescue boats from Cuba and Florida finally arrived—a few *weeks* later.

Back in Spain King Philip was mourning the tragedy. But he was also very concerned about the great fortune that was lost when those ships sank. So he sent soldiers to try to retrieve the precious cargo.

They forced local natives to dive down to

search for the treasure, tying rocks to their ankles to help them sink! Once the divers came back to the surface, they were searched to make sure they didn't steal any of the loot.

The divers did a great job recovering quite a bit of the lost treasure—about 5 million pieces! Yet more than 3 million objects were still lost along forty miles of ocean waters. Word spread and people flocked to Florida to try to find the riches themselves.

Not everyone was an innocent person just looking to strike gold. Some who came were thieves and pirates, including a couple of ships ordered by the king of Jamaica. He overtook the Spanish soldiers' camp and went home with 350,000 pieces of their valuable treasure. Even today, it's said that millions of dollars' worth of valuables are still hidden at the bottom of the ocean here in Florida.

More than just gold and pearls, the area is

even richer in spirits as the shore has become a mass cemetery for all who died there and whose bones are buried nearly as far down as the lost treasure. In fact, people who go today trying to find some of the buried goods say that they feel like a pair of eyes may be watching them as they walk along the beach.

Others see strange lights in the water even with no boats nearby, and some hear very clear whispers, crying, and moaning in the distance. The sandy areas surrounding this part of the Treasure Coast are known as haunted beaches as many have taken photos with strange shadow figures that appear in the image or hear voices still asking for help all these years later.

CHAPTER 3

The Driftwood Resort

If there's one ghost that everyone around the Treasure Coast knows by name, it's good old Waldo Sexton. If his name wasn't strange enough, Waldo's personality was even more bizarre.

He first came to the area known as Vero Beach in the year 1914. Waldo had been born and raised in Indiana and went to Purdue University where he studied agriculture and farming. His work brought him to Florida, and he loved it so much that he stayed, bought some land, and started planting citrus trees. He was such a great farmer—he discovered a way to raise sturdier cows that could hold up to Florida summers—that the US government named an avocado type after him! As Waldo got older and the Great Depression made it harder for him to farm, he became a realtor and was very successful in that job, too. But all that was a bit too "normal" for this very over-the-top man.

Soon he partnered with a guy named Arthur McKee to open a big attraction for tourists called McKee Jungle Gardens. (It was as fun as it sounds!) With a huge plot of land stretching eighty acres, they first focused on very interesting plants—from pretty water lilies and orchid flowers to exotic trees you couldn't normally find in the US. Then the animals came—there was a large bird population, some friendly monkeys, and even an alligator named Ole Mac who would greet visitors who stopped by the Jungle Gardens. When they did, Waldo Sexton would be there to say hi too, usually with a monkey sitting on his shoulders. The park was so popular it brought in about 100,000 people a year in the days before Disney came to Florida. People loved coming to the Jungle Gardens with their friends and family. But when Walt Disney World opened in 1971, it was too much competition for the Jungle Gardens, which eventually closed in 1976. But that didn't stop Waldo.

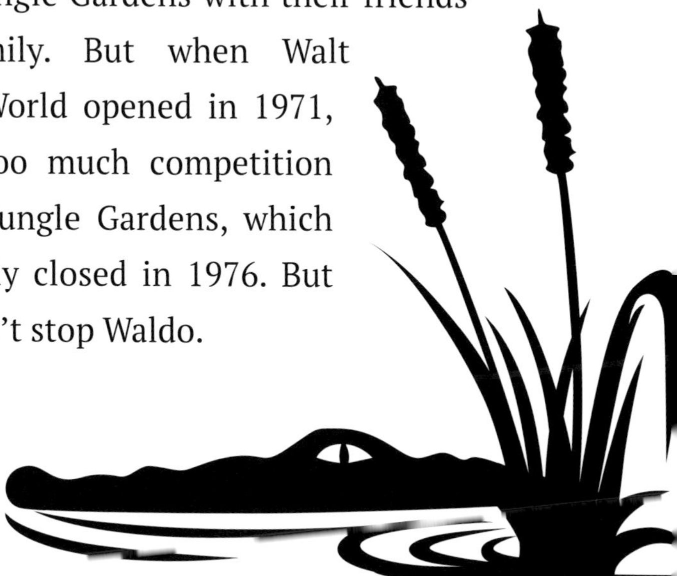

He started to focus on a new place he'd call the Driftwood Inn. Originally, he built it in the 1930s as a vacation home for his family. But as more and more friends in the community came to spend time at this breezy resort, he decided to open it up to the public. In addition to rooms to stay in overnight, he added a couple of restaurants—and the best part is, he decorated it from top to bottom with all of his unusual collectibles. The walls were overflowing with shells from the beaches, antiques from shipwrecks, wood he'd rescued from abandoned buildings, and lots and lots of bells. He loved the sound of bells. Waldo made the place look and feel just as odd as he was, and here's where the story takes a dark turn.

Like any human being, Waldo knew he would die some day. In anticipation of it happening, he decided to build a manmade mountain near his Driftwood Resort, which was to be his final resting spot. He wanted to be buried beneath it. Waldo built it up very high–perhaps inspired by what the Ais people did with their burial mounds—and added stairs and a collection of colorful tiles he collected in his many shopping expeditions.

On the very tippy top he had two chairs and a cross—no one really knows why. But everyone was intrigued, and many tried to climb to the top and take a rest once they did. Waldo lived to a very ripe old age of 82, and with all the time that passed, his mountain fell into bad shape. People stole the tiles, and the structure started to fall apart. When he did die, Waldo's family chose not to honor what he requested for his final plans and instead buried him in a graveyard near other family members. In fact, Waldo's son even had the mountain torn down so he could use the soil to save the Driftwood property from flooding during one of Florida's bad hurricanes. Now you may have heard someone before say that if their family didn't do what they asked when they died, they'd "come back to haunt them." Well, guess who did just that?

Three people tried to buy the property after Waldo died, and each one met a very grave ending. One of them had a massive heart attack and died before they could sign the papers. Another *did* sign the papers but died in a plane crash on the way home. The third one who tried to buy the property lost all his money and went bankrupt. It seemed Waldo didn't want anyone else to own the Driftwood, and he made sure to put a stop to it, even from the afterlife.

The Driftwood is still running today, but the latest owner was smart. She decided to keep the odd look of the building just the way Waldo likes it, and she greets him every day. It seems that being acknowledged has made him happy—the dark turn of events have stopped. Though it's said Waldo still sticks around.

He died in 1967 but for more than fifty years he has been "greeting" people who still come to this very popular spot. On a ghost tour that comes through the Driftwood, Waldo has many times showed he likes certain people by giving them a forceful shove on their shoulder. Some even almost fell because he pushed them so hard! Other guests will say they see a ghost-like figure in a hat and suspenders (Waldo's favorite outfit) walking down by the beach. But when they try to go talk to him, he vanishes into thin air. If you try to take a photo here, you will likely see a big glowing orb or shadowy figure—a "dead" giveaway that Waldo wants to say hi.

CHAPTER 4

The Ocean Grill

Ghosts must really like to eat out because there's another very haunted restaurant in the Treasure Coast, called the Ocean Grill. Although, it could also be because Waldo Sexton had his hands on this place, too. Not too far from where the Driftwood still stands, the Ocean Grill was opened by Waldo in 1932. Like his other spot, it's situated along the beach where people can dine and look out over the water as they eat. When he first opened it, Waldo wanted it to be a fast and convenient hot dog stand. Although after ten years of business, he decided to turn it into a larger restaurant. Inside were all his same odd collectibles decorating the walls and large stained-glass figurines.

When he made it into a more formal restaurant in 1941, Waldo decided to focus on the Driftwood instead, and he let a pair of new owners take care of the Ocean Grill. They were a couple from Germany named Russ and Emma Adler. Around this time, however, the US entered World War II, and there were a lot of anti-German feelings in the US. People associated the German couple with the war. Some even thought that Russ and Emma were German spies who were giving secret info to the submarines stationed nearby. And the next thing you know, the Adlers were gone!

They disappeared into the night—no one knows what happened to them. Perhaps they escaped on their own. Or maybe something darker happened to them. But they were never seen again.

The strange occurrences didn't stop there, though. Just a few days after the Adlers suddenly disappeared, on May 6, 1942, there were three attacks by the German U-333 Submarine very close to Vero Beach (where the Driftwood and Ocean Grill are located). The submarine destroyed a couple of American oil tankers and a cargo ship. Sadly, a number of people, including sailors and Naval officers,

died during the attacks. Residents were very shaken up. They couldn't believe the war had come so close to their home turf in the Treasure Coast. With these events and the Adlers gone, Waldo Sexton re-emerged and decided to make the Ocean Grill into offices for Naval officers so they could conduct missions in a safe space. However, it all seemed very much like a coincidence with the timing—perhaps the Adlers really were spies. We may never know!

After the war ended, another group of shady characters took over the Ocean Grill—a bunch of mobsters and mafia men like you might see in the movies. Given the restaurant's closeness to the water, and knowing that mobsters sometimes liked to take victims "out to sea," it was a prime spot for them. Though no customers dared step foot in the restaurant at this time, afraid they might meet the same cruel ending!

The Ocean Grill is still open today, run by a very nice family who welcomes anyone to come get a bite. But with all the sadness, mysterious disappearances, and deaths at the hands of the war or the mob, you can only imagine the Ocean Grill is full of paranormal energy from the restless spirits.

CHAPTER 5

The Sunrise Theatre

There's a part of the Treasure Coast known as Fort Pierce, or the "Sunrise City," and it's one of the oldest parts of town. Back in the day, it looked and felt like the Wild West with lots of railroads and cattle. It was where a lot of boaters and fishermen did their business. But over time it was spruced up and renovated as many people from the northern part of the US came to Florida to visit and enjoy all the sunshine. Today, Fort Pierce is a lovely place that honors its historic past.

One of its main attractions is the beautiful Sunrise Theatre that was built in the 1920s. It has a vintage look, though today it welcomes modern music acts for concerts as well as top-notch theater productions. It was opened by wealthy businessman Rupert Koblegard who saw potential for Fort Pierce being less of a "cow town" and more as a place for culture and the arts.

At the time it opened in 1923, it was one of the classiest and prettiest theaters in this part of the country. There was a big parade with a band and dancing in the streets to celebrate its opening, and the first event it offered the townsfolk was then a new attraction—moving pictures, or movies. The first one they showed was the old silent black-and-white Charlie Chaplin film, *The Vagabond*.

For years after it was *the* gathering place in town where people would come together for a show, whether it was a daredevil cowboy or a troupe of dancers. Even as the Great Depression took hold, the Sunrise Theatre still did great business. People needed entertainment to make themselves feel better and bring some relief from the hard times they were experiencing. The officers from the nearby naval base who worked from the Ocean Grill were also frequent visitors to the theater. It's said that even some of those German submarine officers were able to once sneak in to see a movie.

But over time, fewer and fewer people were coming through the doors at the Sunrise as the area around the Treasure Coast started developing and offering more exciting and modern entertainment options. Fort Pierce also started becoming a rougher neighborhood that many did not want to spend too much time in. So by 1983, the theater closed its doors, but perhaps not everyone left the building when it did. Some people reported they could see dark shadowy figures in the windows when looking in, and others who were inside would hear unexplained knocking on the walls, almost as if the spirits wanted to be let out.

In 2006, the Sunrise was set to reopen after millions of dollars went into updating it. But even then, the workers who were handling the construction of the building felt very strange things happening too. They'd see objects and

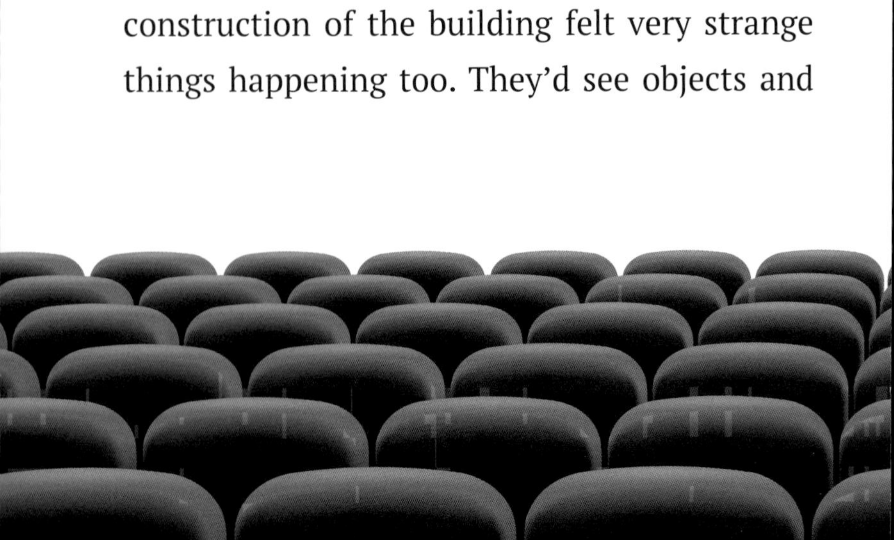

mysterious figures moving about the building and hear strange noises at all hours of the day. Even a paranormal group was invited to see if they could understand any of this strange activity. As soon as they were inside, all their battery power was drained on their phones and devices, and they saw doors opening and closing by themselves. Some think that the ghost that haunts the place is that of Robert Koblegard who dreamed up the place and helped make it a reality back in the 1920s. Maybe he just still wants to be the star of the show!

CHAPTER 6

The Boston House

If you're looking for a *really* haunted house in the Treasure Coast, you'll surely find one in the Boston House, named for being close to Fort Pierce's famed Boston Avenue. It was originally the home of a man named William Turpin Jones and his family. William worked for the railroad company in Florida, and he built the house in 1909, but many think the money used to do so was cursed. You see, William was involved in two very bad train accidents that almost took his life—and the money he got from the insurance settlements he then used to make his home. The first accident was when his train was traveling over dynamite that was left on the tracks and caused the train to explode! And another was when his train crashed head-on with another locomotive—William was only able to survive because he saw it happening and jumped into a body of water near the tracks before the crash! After these terrible incidents, he decided to leave the railroad company and became a realtor. He eventually found a job as the town's sheriff.

While William and his family lived in the Boston House, a few terrible things happened that forever changed them. First, there was the time in 1913 when William's son Fred had just become engaged to his future bride, Ada. After a big celebration at the family home, Fred, his fiancée, her sister Nola, and another friend, Raymond, went out for a motorcycle ride. Fred and Raymond each drove a bike while Ada and Nola held on tight behind them. It was a dark night, and they were on a very winding road. The two motorcycles lost control and ended up crashing. Sadly, Nola died from her injuries.

Just five years later, in 1918, tragedy struck the family again. William's ten-year-old son, Clifford, and his friend, also named William, were playing in the living room. They happened to find a loaded gun. Thinking it was just a prop toy, they played around with it, but soon the gun fired for real, and a bullet hit little Willy in the stomach. He too lost his life from his injuries. It was almost like the house itself was causing these horrible events to happen.

When the Great Depression hit in the next decade, William Turpin Jones lost everything, and he was forced to sell the Boston House. It went through a few owners over the decades. First it was the private home of Rose Whitney and her elderly sister who both died in the home after suffering from long illnesses. Then the house was taken over as offices for an engineering firm called Wood, Beard, and Associates until 1976.

But perhaps its most interesting ownership was when Leonard and Diane Cottem took the building over and turned it into a bed-and-breakfast. But not just any cozy B&B. The husband and wife were very interested in the supernatural and black magic, and they promoted the house as being haunted and even held seances with guests to try to conjure up the spirits inside, which of course has only made those ghosts more active.

One very frequent ghostly visitor is that of a woman named Aleacon Perkins. Everyone knows when they see her because she has very pretty red hair that always stands out. The legend goes that she and her husband and their young son Tim booked a night at the bed-and-breakfast, and the boys were looking forward to a fishing trip the next day. When they left the following morning, there was an unexpected Florida storm and the boys never returned home. Very worried that something happened to them, Aleacon called the police who conducted a search and sadly found the overturned fishing boat and the husband's lifeless body. To this day, the remains of little Tim have never been found. Aleacon was devastated, and it's said that on very stormy nights, people can see her standing at one of the upstairs windows in the Boston House waiting for her boys to come back to her. Even when psychics have come to the house, she's one of the first they make contact with from the spirit world.

But she's not the only one. Other reported hauntings inside the Boston House—which today is a law firm—include stories of employees who hear nonstop laughter in some of the rooms or can hear a woman wailing at the top of her lungs. Others have seen windows open and close when no one is around and

even smell very strong perfume even when they're alone. Though, it doesn't happen often, as no one ever likes to be by themselves in the Boston House!

CHAPTER 7

The Ghost Ship

Ghosts don't always have to take on a human form. Sometimes they can be haunted objects, too. In the case of the Treasure Coast, some have said that on a really dark night, if you look out over the water of the St. Lucie River, you might even see a ghost ship traveling slowly to shore! Many believe the ship is being steered by none other than the famous pirate Black Caesar who used to travel these same waters hundreds of years ago. He was a giant figure, standing very tall with big muscles and, even in life, many people were afraid of him.

Originally, Black Caesar was a very brave war chief in Africa. He was so successful because he was very intelligent and knew how to trick the enemy he was fighting. Once he decided to live as a pirate, he used the same trickery—often traveling the St. Lucie River because it winded around many bends. That offered sneaky hiding places from the Spanish who passed through the area while transporting jewels and other valuables back to Europe.

One day, though, Black Caesar got a taste of his own medicine. Another group of mischievous pirates told the towering man and his crew of outlaws that if they came on board their ship, they'd be rewarded with lots of expensive goods. Believing the promise,

Black Caesar brought his team aboard, but immediately they were taken prisoner and chained below deck. The very charming man he was, Black Caesar became friends with one of the crewmen, and one day during a very bad hurricane that made the boat unsteady as it traveled through the Florida waters, they were able to overtake the ship. They found the captain's weapons and threatened his life. The captain surrendered to them. Black Caesar and the traitor crewman stole valuables from the ship and took off in a rowboat, somehow surviving the hurricane-force winds and miraculously making it to shore alive.

Once on shore they set up a new home base and worked with local native people to come up with some more tricks to steal more loot. They decided that when they would see a ship coming close to shore, they'd travel to meet them in their rowboat and lie to the crew, telling them they were stranded at sea. Once the crew allowed them to find safety on board, Black Caesar and his sidekick would overtake the ship and threaten the crew. The pair did this for years, even tempting many of the underpaid sailors to join their thievery. One day, however, Black Caesar got into a fight with his partner, and he killed him!

Being the leader of the pack, Black Caesar only became more powerful, eventually overtaking a whole island where he could hold people captive and continue to attack boats to steal their treasures. This worked especially well during the Disaster of 1715, when King

Philip V lost so much treasure along the coast. When the pirates swarmed to the Treasure Coast to search for the exotic jewels and valuables that sunk to the bottom of the ocean, Black Caesar was there among them.

Eventually, though, Black Caesar's life of crime caught up with him, and he was arrested and sentenced to death by hanging. Perhaps because he died such a terrible death,

Black Caesar is said to still travel the waters. One time, a man named Wallace Stevens—a resident of the nearby town of Stuart—wrote for the local paper about the strange thing he saw happening in the water in 1931. He swore he once saw a "phantom ship" rocking on the waves under the moonlight. The thing that struck Wallace as odd was that the ship had no light guiding it, and it traveled too fast to be realistically possible, especially without the sound of any engine powering it. Not only that, but the ship looked old-fashioned, like ancient boats he'd only seen in history books and never in real life. And there was no one on board! After screaming for the ship to "watch out!" as it was about to collide with his, Wallace desperately maneuvered his boat out of its path—and when he turned back around, the ghost ship was mysteriously gone, like it had never even existed. Was it Black Ceasar's ship? Or another pirate's? I guess we'll never know.

CHAPTER 8

The Leach Mansion

You'll never find a doormat reading "Home Sweet Home" at the Leach Mansion in Jensen Beach, Florida. Other than how it looks—like a supersized bright white palace straight out of old Hollywood—there's nothing sweet about this home. Perched high atop a sandy hill, the mansion was abandoned for many years. And like you might see in the movies, many urban legends have swirled about the strange goings on inside its walls. And if those walls could talk, they'd tell several very interesting stories!

Originally, an adventurous man named William H. Racey bought the property in the 1850s as part of a purchase of hundreds of acres

of land. William wanted to create a popular city in Florida that would attract tourists. But he saved one spot for himself—this spot high atop the mountain. He named it Mount Elizabeth in honor of his mother, and he planned to build his retirement home at the very top.

But there was one problem. As you might already be thinking, doesn't that sound like those really high burial mounds that the Ais native tribes created? You are absolutely right. The site of William's future home was also the site of an ancient mound where the Ais may have done many of their rituals. Maybe William didn't know it at the time, but he and everyone else after him soon found out just how cursed this land was. William died in 1874 before he could build his retirement paradise and another man, Benjamin Darling, bought the property years later. Benjamin was successful building a home where he lived with his family for about ten years. But within that time, William Racey's son Charles discovered that the property wasn't sold correctly and was still in his name. He rightfully took back what was owed to him. Charles then expanded on the house and built the gorgeous three-story mansion his dad always wanted. He held fancy parties and enjoyed lots of company, but in 1923, the luxurious house burned to the ground.

Thinking the plot of land might be cursed, the Racey family moved away, and the property was bought by Willaford Ransom Leach—he and his wife had lots of money (she was part of the family that owned Coca-Cola!), and they used their funds to build the Leach Mansion that stands proud today. It has eight fireplaces, lots of balconies and a swimming pool so big that the Red Cross has used it for training people! But, after yet another of those bad

Florida hurricanes and a big disagreement with the local town government about how much taxes they should have to pay, the Leaches decided to sell the house to the Catholic Church for a mere $75,000 (far, far less than what it was actually worth). The church used it as a center to train and house nuns—nothing too spooky happened during this time, maybe because the spirits didn't want to bother people so holy! But later, when the mansion was sold yet again to the Florida Institute of Technology for use as classroom space, funny things started acting up in the house.

One night a professor had to stay late in the building after giving an exam to her students. She was the only one left behind, and the school staff had already turned the lights out, leaving her alone to walk down the dark, empty hallways by herself. Feeling that someone was behind her, she quickly turned around to see a terrifying figure of a man looming near her. He was wearing a long coat and hat and just stood there staring at her! She tried to be friendly and say hello, but he didn't move. She then advanced quickly towards the stairs to make her quick getaway and, as she did, she watched the man disappear right before her eyes. In no surprise, the teacher quit her job and never returned to Leach Mansion.

After the Florida college moved out, the building again was abandoned for some time. People would sometimes sneak in to see if they could feel anything strange or connect with spirits—and when they did, they would feel cold spots that sent shivers down their spines or see glowing orbs moving in the distance that were just as spooky. In the auditorium, many would see shadowy figures moving about the seats—this room in particular is where a lot of the haunted activity happened.

Sometimes even soft piano music could be heard playing or a faint choir might be singing in the background.

Today, Leach Mansion looks like its glorious old self after many millions of dollars were put into renovating it. When workers were completing the job, they dug so far into the ground they found pottery relics that experts said dated back more than 4,000 years! So, no matter how many years go by, the Ais people have made sure to make their presence known in more ways than one.

CHAPTER 9

Gilbert's Bar House of Refuge

Watch your back if you're at Gilbert's on a night with a full moon! Many strange things have happened here when the moon hangs low, as if it were a light drawing the spirits to come out and frolic in full view. This modest structure is more than 140 years old—it's not only the oldest building but it's also considered one of the most haunted houses on Florida's east coast. Today it's a museum that shows what the area was like back in the pioneer days before railroads and cars and people moved in to make it a real city.

Gilbert's Bar House of Refuge dates all the way back to the times of the American Civil War. After the war ended, people started migrating to different parts of the country. One area that hadn't been built up yet was the coastline of Florida. Despite it seeming easy to get to, the coast of Florida has some treacherous waters. Early explorers discovered that the hard way, sometimes crashing their ships. Survivors would have no place to go to find shelter, food, or help.

That was until 1875 when the US Lifesaving Service was started by the government, and they built "houses of refuge" like Gilbert's. At these refuges, shipwreck victims could find resources and heal before moving on their journey again. Each had a housekeeper who, with her family, would search the beaches after every storm, to make sure no one was in trouble and, if so, rescue them. Sometimes there were so many victims that the housekeeper had to cook the largest amount of soup she could to feed the victims—and she'd have to use her bathtub to do so!

Of the many rescue houses that were built along the coast, Gilbert's is the only one remaining, and it's quite the historical treasure. One of the other reasons is because the site—like so many others in this book—was one of the ancient Ais tribesmen and women from more than 2,000 years ago! We know this because, after two devastating hurricanes in the past twenty years washed away a lot of the surface near the house, skeletal remains and relics associated with the Ais were unearthed.

The site was then blessed by a Native American shaman (like a priest), but it hasn't stopped the spirits from lingering. On those nights with a full moon, lights will suddenly shine bright near the house even though no one is there to flicker them on, and some distant voices can be heard crying out into the night sky.

One other man who may be haunting the house is Don Pedro Gibert—in fact, it's his name (with an "L" added in) that inspired Gilbert's Bar House of Refuge. Don Pedro was not a very good man. He was one of the infamous pirates who threatened the waters in the early 19th century. Originally from Colombia, he found his way to Florida with his ship, the *Panda*, and his trick was to hide the vessel between large hills on Hutchinson Island—and then he'd use a telescope to search for other boats approaching. When he found one, he'd immediately attack the crew and lock them up, take over the ship, loot all the possessions, and then he'd set the ship on fire so no one survived!

Eventually Don Pedro and his criminal crew were arrested and went on trial in Boston where 20,000 people showed up to see the outcome. Back in those days, pirate trials were a form of entertainment like movies or a sports game. The men were sentenced to death by hanging in the town square. Even more people came to watch their awful ending. But even though he died 150-plus years ago, it's said Don Pedro's ghost remains. Again, on those full moon nights, some see a dark vessel sailing along the waters with red lights that look like demon eyes.

A couple of other spirits that may be haunting Gilbert's Bar House of Refuge are that of Captain Louie and Susan Bessey. After the US Coast Guard was formed around the time of World War II, the House of Refuge was used as a watchtower by the military looking for any suspicious boats or aircraft from enemy territories. However, when the war ended, the government no longer took care of the house and in moved Captain Louie.

The once-great sailor had no home so he used the House of Refuge as shelter, and he was very well liked by people in the community who'd bring food for him and offer rides into town when he needed to go somewhere. It's said he could tell some really good stories too, so people liked being around him. Sadly, on one night in 1958, there was a huge fire reported in the area and, later, the remains of Captain Louie were found in the ashes. Today, he still seems to be his same playful self when visitors come by. He might laugh in your ear or pull on your shirt or even knock on the walls of the House of Refuge just to mess with you.

But rest assured, he loves visitors and means no harm.

Susan Bessey is another known spirit. She was the real-life wife of one of the innkeepers, Hubert Bessey, up until 1902. Susan was a very caring person who tried to make shipwreck victims comfortable by keeping the house clean, tending to their wounds, and cooking for them when they were at the House of Refuge. Even today, her ghostly figure can be seen in an upstairs window looking out to sea and making sure no one is out there who needs her help. And sometimes the rich aroma of a hearty soup can be smelled from the kitchen even though it's no longer in operation—Susan may still be stirring a pot for the next group to come stay awhile.

CHAPTER 10

The Ashley Gang

Chicago is not the only place famous for its history of mobsters like Al Capone. In Florida, the most notorious mobster is a man named John Ashley—and much like the bad guys that make Chicago so haunted, John does the same on the Treasure Coast. John grew up in the Roaring '20s, the time before the Great Depression when life was pretty good for people. And even though Prohibition was going on (that's when the government didn't allow the sale of alcohol), people got around the rules. People like John Ashley—who became trapped in a world of crime. It's said that John and his band of brothers, called the Ashley Gang, robbed nearly forty banks and stole more than $1 million!

They were fugitives wanted by the police for a long time. And things only got worse when John went on a hunting trip with a friend from the Seminole Indian tribe. Something very bad happened on that trip and only John returned home, though he spoke nothing of it. But when his friend's body was later discovered, John was charged with murder.

Sheriff George Baker of Gomez (where the Ashleys lived) sent officers to arrest John, but he and his gang attacked them and sent the sheriff a threatening message to never return. It started a war between Sheriff Baker and the

Ashley family that lasted for a long while—even between multiple generations of the families.

Part of the problem was that the Ashley family seemed just as powerful as the police and were good at escaping them. It's said that John escaped jail *three* times after being locked up for his crimes. And his brother Bob even went to break him free from jail once, a bad idea that erupted into a street shootout with the cops. Bob died. And because the townsfolk were so scared of the Ashleys, the police held a parade where they took Bob's body into the streets so people could see he was actually dead. How crazy is that?

But John truly didn't think he was the "bad guy." He figured he was stealing from the rich (like the insurance companies and banks) to give back to the

hardworking poor people in Florida. And he was a hero to many of them. He also employed people in his homegrown whiskey business. Despite that business being illegal (because of Prohibition), it still provided jobs. John helped local folks earn a salary to feed their families and pay their bills.

For this reason, John Ashley was pretty well loved by the tight-knit community. Though, he was still hated by police, especially the new Sheriff Bob Baker—son of Sheriff George Baker. Sheriff Bob hated John for what he did to his father and also because John married the woman he loved. So, after getting top secret info out of one of John's workers at the whiskey plant, Sheriff Bob sent fifty men on horseback to try to kill John and his wife, Laura. The couple was able to escape police yet again, though several of their associates were killed in the gunfire.

Finally, under the full moon of Halloween night in 1924, John and three prominent members of the Ashley Gang met their fateful end. Cops had set up roadblocks on a bridge the gang was trying to cross, and after a tense meeting, the four outlaws were shot dead on the spot.

It's said that John and his Gang are still trying to seek revenge for their murder, even from the afterlife. Many of the places they used to visit have some very intense energy, including the bridge where they died. Every year on November 1, the morning after the anniversary of their deaths, people have reported seeing four pools of blood in the exact spots where the four men died. No one can explain it—could it be John and his men reminding people of the brutal way they died that night?

It's also said that, at the cemetery where

the Ashley family is buried, there has been some unusual activity and residents have often complained about strange goings on that they could see from their windows. They'd see lights flickering on and off almost like flashlights, even when the cemetery was shut down for the night. And they'd hear noises that sounded more like humans than animals.

When complaints poured in, the security guards that worked for the graveyard would go to check the grounds and find nothing. This would happen nightly until finally trees and fences were built to create a big line of separation from the real world and the spirit world. But, just like when they were alive, the Ashleys seem to escape the realm they are in and keep causing havoc.

CHAPTER 11

The Ghosts of Port Salerno

It's long been known that sailors and fishermen are some very superstitious people who believe that nothing is left to fate—which perhaps explains why Port Salerno in the Treasure Coast is so haunted. In the 19th century, the town was full of men who lived by the sea and made their living catching fish to sell, and at night they'd use their money at the local bars which could get kind of rowdy. Yet, the history of Port Salerno also has another interesting twist with more connections to the otherworld.

Originally this small pocket of land had no name, but it soon got one thanks to a man named Henry Morrison Flagler who many see as one of the main developers of the Treasure Coast. Henry was the founder of the Florida East Coast Railway, which made travel possible throughout the remote area and brought more people to town who eventually settled into living and working there. He also previously worked in New York with the Rockefeller family and the Standard Oil business.

Henry's wife, Mary, was quite sick—diagnosed with an awful disease called tuberculosis—and he tried moving the family from New York south to Florida to see if the warm weather and sunshine might make her feel better. It didn't exactly work, and Henry hired a nurse named Alice to watch over

Mary while he went to his many meetings and business trips. Sadly, Mary didn't live for very long. Henry and his son had both become quite fond of Alice, so after Mary died, Henry married Alice. With Henry gone so much of the time, Alice became very lonely which soon influenced her state of mind.

Around this time, a friend gave Alice a Ouija board which Alice used to communicate with the dead. Her stories about all the ghosts she was meeting and her interest in voodoo and tarot cards made Henry worry. In those times, people with psychic abilities were thought of as crazy though it was not the case.

Henry sought out therapists for Alice but, after Alice tried to stab one with a pair of scissors, she was

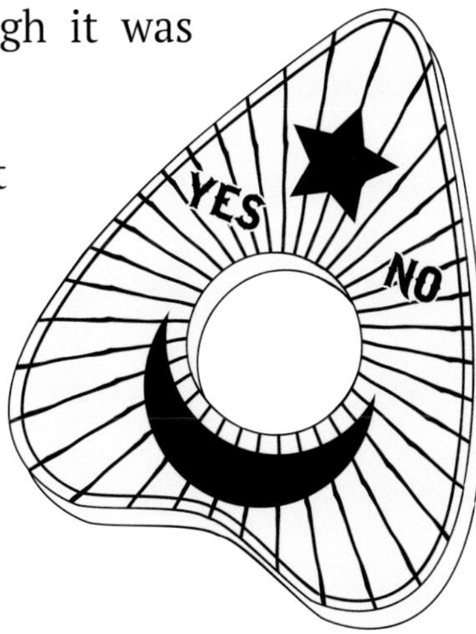

committed to a hospital and locked away for the rest of her life. Henry then changed the law himself to legally divorce Alice. But perhaps he felt guilty about his poor treatment of his once beloved wife. He decided to name the part of town where they lived Alicia in honor of her. It's said Alice still looms over the town—perhaps wanting people to know she wasn't lying when she said she was able to connect with the afterlife by making her spirit so present now.

Alice is not the only one to haunt these parts now known officially as Port Salerno. Many of the famed superstitious fishermen who once called the port home still linger. One of them is Pompano Chuck Solmer who was one of the best fish catchers of his day. He also loved animals so very much that he kept twelve dogs as pets, even when he was living out of his car! Today he's considered the spiritual guide for animals in Port Salerno, keeping a watchful eye over all the furry friends in the wilderness.

"Dirty" Freddie is another interesting ghost. In real life, Freddie Gladwish was a successful engineer. But he didn't like all the stress of his job so one day he quit and decided to live on a boat. He didn't have many frills or clothes or shoes for that matter! But he did have one suit he'd wear on Saturday nights when he'd dock his vessel and go into town to meet women. Sadly, Freddie was hit and killed by a drunk driver late one night. But many women today say they still feel strange things on Saturday nights when they go out to restaurants, such as a hand that touches their shoulder, or someone's breath on their ear like he's trying to whisper words of flattery.

Yet perhaps the saddest ghost story here is that of the "Lady in White" who has haunted residents and visitors for many years. Her real name was Mary, and she was as happy as any young woman could be. She had just married her sweetheart, Roger, in a huge wedding with lots of family and friends around her. The couple packed their car, headed for the train station to begin their honeymoon and their new life together.

But suddenly, like it often happens in Florida, a huge surprise storm rolled in and sheets of rain fell hard and fast. Roger lost control of the car and it spun around several times before it hit a tree head on. Roger, though bloody and hurt, was able to get out of the car. But when he went around to the passenger side and opened the door, he found Mary's lifeless body with blood covering her pristine white wedding dress. To this day, many have reported driving on this same highway seeing a young woman walking alongside the road crying and wearing a white dress soaked with blood. She wanders aimlessly, looking for the future she never got to have.

CHAPTER 12

The Abandoned Cemetery

Sometimes when people are in the Treasure Coast really looking for treasure, they find something even more priceless. This is what happened to a man named Jim. One day while in a quiet part of town called Hobe Sound, he was using a GPS tracker on his phone that allowed him to detect if there were any buried valuables underground. As he stepped through some weeds to get to a clearing, his foot hit a hidden tombstone. It looked to be very old, so much so that he couldn't even make out the name engraved in it. As he looked around, he found three more graves that looked alike, and Jim was pretty sure he had somehow come upon an abandoned cemetery where people were still buried but with no one to tend to it.

Jim was disturbed by what he found and the fact that people could just be buried and forgotten about—it seemed like a sad way to rest for eternity. And so he became obsessed with finding out more about the cemetery and the people who called it their final home.

When he researched more and found official documents at the library, he discovered the cemetery was part of an old Africa Methodist Episcopal church attended by many African American residents. These graves were created around the 1930s, well before the Civil Rights Movement of the 1960s, so Jim was sure it was a segregated cemetery, meaning it was meant only for Black families. White families would be buried somewhere else, in a white-only cemetery.

Back when these graves were created, the Black community would gather together for Sunday services and bury their deceased in the little cemetery next to their church.

Sadly, years later, the church was burned to the ground by a group of vandals, and as the land near it became more and more developed, the cemetery was largely forgotten and left to grow wildly. That is, until Jim found it.

He was hearing something in his head telling him to go to the graveyard one more time, and so he made the trek out, bringing his Beagle, Jip, with him. As Jim was examining more of the gravestones, the small dog ran after something in a row of trees and started digging. Jim moved closer to get Jip out of the mess he was creating, and then he saw it—a real human skull on the ground with its eye sockets staring up at him!

It made no sense—there were no other bones near it. Jim thought maybe it was misplaced somehow, and his instinct was to take it with him. He carried the skull under his arm back to his car and wrapped it in a blanket and placed it on the floor of the backseat. As he was driving home, Jim wasn't far from the cemetery when he got the very terrifying feeling he was not alone. Add to that the fact that Jip was barking like crazy, his fur standing up in horror. As Jim looked into his rearview mirror, suddenly he saw a hollow face staring back at him, peeking through strands of long dark hair covered in dirty leaves. The person was sitting in his backseat!

Jim almost lost control of his car in that moment, skidding over to the side of the road.

When he stopped, he looked back again, and the person was gone. As he started to make his way back on the road, that's when he heard a voice whisper, "Take me home." Jim made a U-turn back in his car and raced back to the cemetery. He put the skull back where he found it and never returned.

CHAPTER 13

Trapper Nelson's Camp

In the middle of a town called Jupiter in the Treasure Coast is a large jungle with low hanging trees, swooping birds of every shape and color, and turtles and alligators galore—as well as the ghost of a man many have called a real-life Tarzan.

The story goes that around the early 1930s, at the height of the Great Depression, there were two brothers Vince and Charlie Nelson and their friend John Dykas who were riding the trains across the country, looking for a place to settle. In Jupiter they found a spot near the beach to set up a camp, and began living off the land.

As you can imagine, it wasn't the best of times, and it was hard living this way. There were a lot of disagreements and fights between the three men, and it got so bad that one day an angry Charlie shot John and killed him. Charlie turned himself into the police and was sentenced to twenty years in prison. Not only did the event take one man's life, but it also caused a deep rift between brothers Charlie and Vince. As Charlie was being hauled away from the courtroom to his jail cell, he turned to the judge and his brother Vince, promising he'd come back some day to kill them both.

With Charlie in jail and John dead, Vince was on his own. He decided to stay in the wilderness and found an abandoned cabin near the Loxahatchee River where he set traps and hunted his food, often trapping racoons, snakes, and even bobcats. He also chopped wood every day to have a heat source to cook his meals.

He wasn't very liked in this part of Florida—being a very large man with a New Jersey accent who barely wore any clothes, he stood out like a sore thumb. He became known to the locals as Trapper Nelson or even Tarzan, "King of the Jungle." Soon, as more visitors started coming to the Treasure Coast, there were tours along the river with guides often stopping at Trapper Nelson's Camp. He played his part well—wearing a snake around his shoulders

and having different animals at his side. He even swung from a rope as boats passed by!

It became such a popular attraction for groups and celebrities (the Boy Scouts did overnight trips here, for example) that he started charging admission. He renamed his camp Trapper Nelson's Zoo and Jungle Garden. One of his frequent visitors and friends was Judge Chillingsworth, the same man who sentenced his brother to prison. They dabbled in card games on the weekends with very important men in town like lawyers and politicians and, through these connections, Trapper Nelson was able to get his hands on a lot of land in the area. Trapper Nelson considered it a "gift," but the whole deal was pretty sketchy—and adding to the mystery was the fact that the judge was the victim of a gruesome murder in 1954.

A few years later, Trapper Nelson

unexplainably closed the camp and posted "no trespassing" signs everywhere. He cut down trees to block tours from traveling down the waterway to visit him. Though no one knows for sure why he did it, it's said that the government was on to him, and "inspectors" would show up at his zoo without notice and make him pay heavy fines. There were also cruel teenagers who would play tricks on him, and hunters were starting to invade the area. Trapper was likely worried about the animals he cared for.

Trapper Nelson was also getting very sick. He complained of constant stomachaches and believed he had cancer but refused to see doctors. In 1968, when Trapper Nelson didn't show up for a lunch with friends, they went to his property to make sure he was okay and sadly found the man's large lifeless body next to a shotgun. Some believed he took his own life. Other people had questions since the scene was very suspicious. Trapper Nelson was very close to signing a deal to sell his land for millions of dollars. Did someone try to kill him for the money? Could it have been his brother Charlie who vowed to kill him and the judge all those years ago? Charlie was released from prison in 1951. Both men were now dead, so perhaps it *was* Charlie?

But, like many of the ghosts in this book, it doesn't appear that Trapper Nelson ever left his home. The local park services took over the area, and when a new park ranger was training, she heard a man's voice in her ear saying, "If I weren't dead, I'd be asking you out." No one else claimed to have heard it but they did say that the Trapper was a big flirt with women.

Another time that same ranger was in her office, and she saw the actual real-size ghost of Trapper Nelson standing in front of her! She was so spooked she called a psychic to come to the grounds to speak with Trapper—and he indeed had a message! There were two Native American burial plots (likely of the ancient Ais people) that he wanted to make sure were being kept safe.

Others have seen the ghost of Trapper Nelson too, like kayakers who swear they see him waving from a dock near the water. Some have heard his voice while walking the property. And one time when workers were repairing the cabin that used to be his house, they found a stash of coins hidden behind some bricks. But when they tried to take them, they were furiously attacked by two giant birds! Trapper Nelson was always a friend of the animals, and it seems they take care of him even in the afterlife.

FLORIDA

Conclusion

The Treasure Coast is a wild place full of real-life treasures, like gold and jewels if you know where to look for them. It's even more rich with countless ghost stories. From pirates to shipwreck victims, gangs and Tarzans, abandoned cemeteries and creepy mansions, there are so many characters and places here that fill up the coast with unexplained experiences. Just remember, as Jim discovered at the abandoned cemetery, if you ever visit the Treasure Coast and find some good loot, you might want to leave it where you found it, unless you want to feel the wrath of the ancient Ais people who still lay claim to their land!

Selena Fragassi is a Chicago-based writer who grew up in a real haunted house and has loved all things paranormal since she had her first experience with a ghost as a teenager. In addition to writing for Spooky America, Selena is a music journalist and has written for such publications as the *Chicago Sun-Times*, *Chicago Tribune*, A.V. Club, Blurt, Paste, Popmatters, Under The Radar and Nylon, among others. She is also working on an upcoming novel about her grandfathers' experiences during World War II.

Check out some of the other Spooky America titles available now!

Spooky America was adapted from the creeptastic Haunted America series for adults. Haunted America explores historical haunts in cities and regions across America. Each book chronicles both the widely known and less-familiar history behind local ghosts and other unexplained mysteries. Here's more from *Ghosts of the Treasure Coast* authors Patricia A. Mesmer and Patrick S. Mesmer:

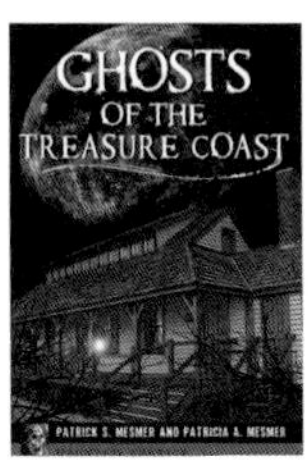